Living Hope

1 & 2 Thessalonians Study Guide

Cover design by Salem Alliance Church
Materials created by Salem Alliance Church
Sarah Morrow, Cary Wood, Laura Scharer, Sam Brown
Printed by permission only
2024

TABLE OF CONTENTS

Preface
What we hope for shapes how we live.

"Paul established the church in Thessalonica during his second missionary journey (about A.D.51)."[1] He wrote 1 & 2 Thessalonians—letters to the church in Tessalonica—from Corinth a short time later in order to encourage the young believers there. Because it was such a young church, the Thessalonian Christians needed to mature in their faith. Believers were being persecuted, and there was a misunderstanding about the second coming of Christ. Many thought that Christ would return immediately and were confused when their loved ones died because they expected that Jesus would return beforehand. Paul both reassured them, corrected their understanding, and strengthened their faith.[2]

Both 1 and 2 Thessalonians illuminate the connection between our future hopes and our daily lives, emphasizing the truth that living in a way that pleases God is an act of worship. Paul's letters to the Thessalonians offer deep insights into how the anticipation of Christ's return should shape our present actions and attitudes, but it is important to note this is done without any legalism or fear.

Written to a young church enduring persecution and uncertainty, these letters are more than just historical records; they remain vibrant and practical for us today. The Thessalonians faced a culture full of distractions and challenges, much like we do. Paul encouraged them—and us—to anchor our lives in the hope of Christ's return. This hope is not a distant dream, but a reality that should influence every aspect of our lives.

Paul's messages remind us that our behavior is a response to God's goodness. Living to please God, which Paul equates with true worship, is not about adhering to legalistic rules but about responding to His grace with integrity, perseverance, and joy. This approach reframes our daily decisions and relationships, guiding us to live fully in light of the promises we profess.

[1] *Life Application Study Bible: NLT.* Zondervan; Tyndale House Publishers, Inc, 2019. 2039

[2] *Life Application Study Bible: NLT.* Zondervan; Tyndale House Publishers, Inc, 2019. 2039

How to Use this Study Guide

Read the Passage Carefully

The passage for each week will not be included in the lesson, but we highly recommend you begin by reading the Bible passage for the lesson thoroughly. Take your time to understand the context and meaning. It's helpful to read it more than once, paying attention to any words or phrases that stand out.

Answer the Questions

After you've read the passage, you'll find questions designed to help you interact with the passage and prompt deeper thinking, reflection, and personal application.

Reflect on the Reflection Prompts

Sprinkled throughout each lesson will be reflections. We encourage you to take time to fully engage with them. Reflecting deeply helps you connect the Scripture to your own life and faith journey, and expand your head knowledge to include heart knowledge. Jot down your reflections, insights, or any questions that arise.

Engage

Each lesson concludes with a section on engagement. This part is designed to help you apply what you've learned in practical ways. It include suggestions for actions or further reflection that can help integrate the lesson into your daily life.

End with Prayer

To close your study, you'll find a prayer included in each lesson. This prayer is meant to be used collectively or individually, and reminds us to ask for guidance, wisdom, and strength as we continue our journey. Feel free to use it as a starting point and add your own personal prayers as well.

Living Examples
Lesson 1
1 Thessalonians 1

Before you begin, start by reading the first chapter of 1 Thessalonians.

In the first chapter of Thessalonians, we see that "... the Thessalonians are facing many burdens, worries, and afflictions, and [we see] Paul's reminder to them that they have been relocated, as it were, into the realm or domain of God and Jesus supplies a kind of identity-anchor on the stormy sea of life."[1]

1. From **1 Thessalonians 1:1-5**, what are some of the things you learn about the church at Thessalonica?

> **"** Paul remembered and commended them for their faithful work, loving deeds, and enduring hope. The word used for endurance or enduring hope is sometimes translated as 'patience/holding your ground' but it's more than what we typically think about being patient. This word includes action— moving forward in spite of resistance.[2] **"**

[1] Gupta, Nijay K. *1-2 Thessalonians: A New Covenant Commentary.* Cascade Books, 2016. 39
[2] Gupta, Nijay K. *1-2 Thessalonians: A New Covenant Commentary.* Cascade Books, 2016. 41

2. How would you describe the difference between patience and endurance?

3. What does enduring hope mean to you?

4. It is important to note that Paul commended the Thessalonian church for not just one thing (only faith or only works, etc.) but rather multiple things. Why do you think it is significant that he mentioned faith, work, love, and hope in his commendation? (See **1 Corinthians 13:13** and **James 2:17-26** as you answer.)

In the next couple of verses, Paul offered a prayer of thanksgiving. It was common for Paul to include prayers in his letters. "The catalyst for his thanksgiving prayer here [**1:3**] was memories. For Paul, remembering was a kind of spiritual discipline (**Romans 1:9**). Looking to God's work among his people (and both God's faithfulness and theirs) was critical for survival in a world full of uncertainties and pressures."[3]

5. How have you utilized the practice of remembering to help you in your faith journey?

Reflection: Take some time to look back and remember some of the things God has done in your life—both big and small. Remember His faithfulness over the years. List some examples. Take time to thank Him.

_____

_____

_____

_____

_____

_____

_____

_____

[3] Gupta, Nijay K. *1-2 Thessalonians: A New Covenant Commentary.* Cascade Books, 2016. 40

In **verse 4**, Paul called the people in the church at Thessalonica "brothers and sisters."

"This is probably Paul's most central image used in 1 Thessalonians to help re-describe their spiritual identity in Messiah Jesus—he refers to them as Christian siblings almost two dozen times across the five chapters. They have been adopted into a single family and household under God the Father (**1:1**) through Jesus the Son (**1:10**), so that Jesus could become 'the firstborn among many brothers and sisters' (**Romans 8:29**)." [4]

"In Paul's world, as in ours, people tended to care for their family in a way not true of outsiders (the proverb 'blood is thicker than water' makes good sense in just about any culture). What happens when Paul links perfect strangers by the bond of siblingship? They are not kin biologically, but the sheer frequency of use of this language from Paul demonstrates that, for him, this was more than a rhetorical device or banal label." [5]

6. How does it sit with you to be likened to a family in this way?

How have you been treated like family in your faith community?

How have you treated others this way?

What could it look like to grow in the area of treating each other like family?

[4] Gupta, Nijay K. *1-2 Thessalonians: A New Covenant Commentary.* Cascade Books, 2016. 41
[5] Gupta, Nijay K. *1-2 Thessalonians: A New Covenant Commentary.* Cascade Books, 2016. 42-43

How can this still be true even when you may disagree?

Jesus prayed for His current disciples and all future generations in **John 17:20-23** saying, *"I am praying not only for these disciples but also for all who will ever believe in me through their message. I pray that they will all be one, just as you and I are one—as you are in me, Father, and I am in you. And may they be in us so that the world will believe you sent me. I have given them the glory you gave me, so they may be one as we are one. I am in them and you are in me. May they experience such perfect unity that the world will know that you sent me and that you love them as much as you love me."*

Like the Thessalonians, how can living this way be an example of Christ to the world?

In **verses 5-9**, Paul highlighted how the Thessalonians' lives reflected Christ and therefore the Word of the Lord had spread everywhere. But he was also quick to ascribe all of their "success" to the work of the Holy Spirit.

7. How would you describe the Holy Spirit's work in the Thessalonian church based on **verses 5-7**?

Reflection: How have you seen the city of Salem (or whatever city you live in) blessed by our church? How have you participated? How would you like to participate?

_____

_____

_____

_____

_____

_____

_____

_____

In **verses 7-8**, "Paul praised this church (no other church received this particular type of praise) because not only were they model believers to an unbelieving world, but they were also examples to other believers."[6]

8. If you were to describe your current influence, would you say it was to believers, non-believers, or both? Why?

9. How can we be good models/examples to both believers and unbelievers?

[6] Barton, Bruce B., and Grant R. Osborne. *1 & 2 Thessalonians: Life Application Commentary*. Tyndale House Publishers, 1999. 24

Paul ended this section of his letter by pointing to the second coming of Jesus, which he emphasized throughout the letter. "Because the Thessalonian church was being persecuted, Paul encouraged them to look forward to the deliverance that Christ would bring. A believer's hope is in the return of Jesus (**Titus 2:13**). Our perspective on life remains incomplete without this hope. Just as surely as Christ was raised from the dead and ascended into heaven, he will return (**Acts 1:11**)."[7]

10. How does thinking about the second coming of Jesus bring you hope?

11. How does that hope shape how you are a living example of Christ today?

[7]*Life Application Study Bible: NLT.* Zondervan; Tyndale House Publishers, Inc, 2019. 2042

Engage

As we go through these letters together, you will notice they are written to a community, not an individual. Paul was encouraging and instructing a group of people who were learning, growing, and enduring together.

As you read and study through 1-2 Thessalonians, think of ways to engage with your current community both through connection and encouragement. Each week, choose one thing from this list to practice as we continue to live out our future hope together.

- Write a note of gratitude or encouragement. Make plans to mail it or send it digitally.

- Ask God to put one person on your heart for prayer. Ask Him, what is on your heart for _____? Then notice any Scriptures, thoughts, or images that come to mind. You may want to share what you prayed and heard with them.

- Go to the Salem Alliance website and refresh your memory about the multiple ways we love and serve each other and our community. Choose a particular ministry to pray for. Consider writing an encouragement card to the point person or leader of that ministry. Pay attention to any ways God might be nudging you to engage with one of the ministries that you see. Use the QR Code below to access the website.

- Take a prayer walk. Ask God to put prayers of blessings on your heart as you walk through a particular neighborhood or area. Also pay attention to any ways that God might be nudging you to engage in acts of service in those areas.

Prayer

End your time together in prayer using Paul's example in **1 Thessalonians 1:2-3**.

2 We always thank God for all of you and pray for you constantly. 3 As we pray to our God and Father about you, we think of your faithful work, your loving deeds, and the enduring hope you have because of our Lord Jesus Christ.

Sermon Notes

PRAYER REQUESTS

Modeled Faith

Lesson 2
1 Thessalonians 2

Before you begin, start by reading the second chapter of 1 Thessalonians.

Paul's visit to the Thessalonian church is recorded in Acts 17. In 1 Thessalonians 2, he reminds the church that he experienced persecution both before he arrived and while he was there. Yet, God gave him courage to share the Good News.

1. What does the word "courage" mean to you?

> **"** When Paul writes about being 'given courage,' this term (*parresiazomai*) carries the idea of public, confident testimony. There is a kind of 'devil-may-care' stubbornness here. Paul is shaping a particular vision that carves out a safe space for Christian identity that can withstand the storms and winds of unfavorable public opinion.[1] **"**

2. Where do you face opposition, fear, or hesitation to living out or sharing the Gospel?

[1]Gupta, Nijay K. *1-2 Thessalonians: A New Covenant Commentary*. Cascade Books, 2016. 53

3. What could it look like to have God-given courage in these areas?

Reflection: Think about times when you've either witnessed or experienced God-given courage. Take time to list some examples. Spend some time in gratitude, thanking God. Invite God to give you courage.

_____

_____

_____

_____

_____

_____

_____

4. In this chapter, it becomes clear that Paul recognized the importance of motivation. In **verses 3-8**, Paul reiterated that he didn't preach for himself or to please people. He shared the Good News to please God. This prompts the question: what motivates you?

Where do you tend to please people rather than God?

A lot of Paul's metaphors in this part of his letter, including being like an infant, nursing mother, and tender father, were designed to share his love and concern for this church. He was pointing to intimate relationships. He wanted them to know that he considered them family, and he was writing to share that they could trust him, his history, his words, and his actions. And they could model their lives after him as he modeled his after Christ. (**1 Corinthians 11:1**)

5. Who do you model your life after?

Who models their life after you?

Reflection: Take time to think about how your life has been shaped by Jesus—your values, your behaviors, and your character. List some examples. Take time to thank God. Invite God to continue shaping you.

_____

_____

_____

_____

_____

_____

_____

In **1 Thessalonians 2:13**, "Paul said that the word of God continued to work in the believers' lives. Paul knew that God's words are not mere sermons or documents but a real source of transforming power."[3]

Hebrews 4:12 says, *"For the word of God is alive and powerful. It is sharper than the sharpest two-edged sword, cutting between soul and spirit, between joint and marrow. It exposes our innermost thoughts and desires."*

6. How have you experienced the Word of God as alive and powerful in your life? In the lives of others?

7. The opposition the Thessalonian Christians were facing came mainly from their own countrymen (**2:14-16**). How did Paul encourage them in their suffering?

Why was this encouragement significant?

Re-read **1 Thessalonians 2:17-20.** Paul shared his desire to return to them and the fact that they brought him so much joy. "The ultimate reward for Paul's ministry was not money, prestige, or fame, but new believers whose lives had been changed by God through the preaching of the Good News. This was why he longed to see them. No matter what ministry God has given you, your highest reward and greatest joy should be those who come to believe in Christ and are growing in him."[4]

8. What does modeling your faith look like in your life? How has this brought you joy?

9. Are there places God is calling you to grow in your ability to share and model your faith? What could that growth look like?

[4] *Life Application Study Bible: NLT.* Zondervan; Tyndale House Publishers, Inc, 2019. 2043

Engage

As we go through these letters together, you will notice they are written to a community, not an individual. Paul was encouraging and instructing a group of people who were learning, growing, and enduring together.

As you read and study through 1-2 Thessalonians, think of ways to engage with your current community both through connection and encouragement. Each week, choose one thing from this list to practice as we continue to live out our future hope together.

- Write a note of gratitude or encouragement. Make plans to mail it or send it digitally.

- Ask God to put one person on your heart for prayer. Ask Him, what is on your heart for _____? Then notice any Scriptures, thoughts, or images that come to mind. You may want to share what you prayed and heard with them.

- Go to the Salem Alliance website and refresh your memory about the multiple ways we love and serve each other and our community. Choose a particular ministry to pray for. Consider writing an encouragement card to the point person or leader of that ministry. Pay attention to any ways God might be nudging you to engage with one of the ministries that you see. Use the QR Code below to access the website.

- Take a prayer walk. Ask God to put prayers of blessings on your heart as you walk through a particular neighborhood or area. Also pay attention to any ways that God might be nudging you to engage in acts of service in those areas.

Prayer

End your time in prayer. Ask God to give you His courage and to allow you to be an example of Christ-likeness throughout your days.

Allow portions of **Psalm 27** to be your prayer.

The LORD is my light and my salvation—
*   so why should I be afraid?*
The LORD is my fortress, protecting me from danger,
*   so why should I tremble?*
Hear me as I pray, O LORD.
*   Be merciful and answer me!*
My heart has heard you say, "Come and talk with me."
*   And my heart responds, "LORD, I am coming."*
Teach me how to live, O LORD.
*   Lead me along the right path,*
Wait patiently for the LORD.
*   Be brave and courageous.*
*   Yes, wait patiently for the LORD.*

Taken from **Psalm 27:1, 7, 8, 11, 14**

Sermon Notes

PRAYER REQUESTS

𝓢𝓽𝓪𝓷𝓭𝓲𝓷𝓰 𝓕𝓲𝓻𝓶
Lesson 3
1 Thessalonians

Before you begin, start by reading the third chapter of 1 Thessalonians.

> When we ended chapter 2, Paul was sharing how heartbroken he was about the suffering of the Thessalonians. Paul and Silas had wanted to return to visit and encourage the Thessalonian church, but they had not been able to get there. Paul revealed that they had been hindered in getting to them by evil spirits.[1] So, Paul decided to send Timothy to Thessolanica to check on them.

1. What was Paul hoping that Timothy would do (there are 3 main things)? **(3:2-3)**

2. In the past (or presently) how has another believer helped you stand firm when you needed encouragement?

Reflection: Ask God: how might You be calling me to be an encouragement to others who are going through troubles or who are feeling shaken?

_____

_____

_____

_____

[1] Barton, Bruce B., and Grant R. Osborne. _1 & 2 Thessalonians: Life Application Commentary._ Tyndale House Publishers, 1999. 45

3. Regarding troubles, what did Paul remind the Thessalonians would be true? (**3:3-4**)

4. In what way is it encouraging to know that troubles are inevitable?

   In what way is it discouraging to know that troubles are inevitable?

5. When Timothy returned to Paul to give him a report, what did he share about the Thessalonians? (**3:6**)

6. In what ways does hearing about someone else's faith encourage you?

7. Do you have a faith story that might encourage someone else?

How would you share it?

_____

_____

_____

_____

_____

_____

_____

Reflection: How have you benefited from the encouragement or ministry of others? Take time to list some examples. Take time to thank God. How could you thank those people this week?

_____

_____

_____

_____

_____

_____

_____

8. The church in Thessalonica was only a few years old and the Christians were newer believers, yet they still encouraged Paul. If new Christians have brought you joy, take some time to thank God for them.

How might you continue to encourage and support those new believers as they grow in their faith?

9. Paul desired to see the Thessalonians again, mentioning that he longed to help fill the gaps in their faith (**3:10**). How have others helped to fill the gaps in your faith?

Paul closed this section of the letter with a prayer for the Thessalonians. *11 May God our Father and our Lord Jesus bring us to you very soon. 12 And may the Lord make your love for one another and for all people grow and overflow, just as our love for you overflows. 13 May he, as a result, make your hearts strong, blameless, and holy as you stand before God our Father when our Lord Jesus comes again with all his holy people. Amen.*

10. What stands out to you in this prayer? (**3:11-13**)

11. What does it look like to be overflowing with love?

Do you think there is always room for more love? Why or why not?

Engage

As we go through these letters together, you will notice they are written to a community, not an individual. Paul was encouraging and instructing a group of people who were learning, growing, and enduring together.

As you read and study through 1-2 Thessalonians, think of ways to engage with your current community both through connection and encouragement. Each week, choose one thing from this list to practice as we continue to live out our future hope together.

- Write a note of gratitude or encouragement. Make plans to mail it or send it digitally.

- Ask God to put one person on your heart for prayer. Ask Him, what is on your heart for _____? Then notice any Scriptures, thoughts, or images that come to mind. You may want to share what you prayed and heard with them.

- Go to the Salem Alliance website and refresh your memory about the multiple ways we love and serve each other and our community. Choose a particular ministry to pray for. Consider writing an encouragement card to the point person or leader of that ministry. Pay attention to any ways God might be nudging you to engage with one of the ministries that you see. Use the QR Code below to access the website.

- Take a prayer walk. Ask God to put prayers of blessings on your heart as you walk through a particular neighborhood or area. Also pay attention to any ways that God might be nudging you to engage in acts of service in those areas.

Prayer

End your time in prayer together. Use the words of **1 Thessalonians 3:12-13** to guide you as you pray for our church as well as churches in our city and even all around the world.

And may the Lord make your love for one another and for all people grow and overflow, just as our love for you overflows. May he, as a result, make your hearts strong, blameless, and holy as you stand before God our Father when our Lord Jesus comes again with all his holy people. Amen.

Sermon Notes

PRAYER REQUESTS

Holy Calling
Lesson 4
1 Thessalonians 4

Before you begin, start by reading the fourth chapter of 1 Thessalonians.

Paul gave the church at Thessalonica a holy calling to holy living. But what does that mean? Holiness is one of God's fundamental characteristics. It describes His absolute purity, moral perfection, and separation from sin. God's holiness defines His otherness and majesty.[1] Our holiness involves being set apart for a special purpose or use by God. This includes the idea of being consecrated or dedicated to God's service, distinguished from the common or profane. [2] "'Calling' includes a commitment on the part of the believers to live holy lives, rather than impure lives. Because it is a call, God is a part of it, promising to help each believer have wisdom, the ability to resist temptation, and the ability to live as God desires." [3]

1. In **1 Thessalonians 4:1**, Paul urged the believers to live in a way that pleases God. How would you describe what it means to live in a way that pleases God?

2. In his exhortation to live in a way that pleases God, Paul acknowledged that they were already living this way, but he encouraged them to do so even more. What areas of your life might God be calling you to surrender or change in order to please Him more fully?

[1] **Isaiah 6:3; Revelation 4:8**
[2] **Exodus 19:6; 1 Peter 2:9**
[3] Barton, Bruce B., and Grant R. Osborne. *1 & 2 Thessalonians: Life Application Commentary.* Tyndale House Publishers, 1999. 59

> **"** When we talk about living to please God, we're really talking about living in a way that reflects His love and grace. It's not about legalistic demands but about letting our lives be an outpouring of the goodness we've received from Him, which transforms every action into worship.[4] **"**

3. How do you see living to please God as an act of worship?

How might that change how you are currently living?

4. How can our behavior reflect His goodness and not come from a place of fear or duty?

[4] Bessey, Sarah. *Out of Sorts: Making Peace with an Evolving Faith*. Howard Books, 2015.

5. Read **1 Thessalonians 4:3-7**. Paul focused his call to holy living in this section of his letter on instructions about sexual wholeness. What do you notice about his instructions?

> 66 God does not forbid sexual sin just to be difficult. He knows its power to destroy us physically and spiritually. No one should underestimate the power of sexual immorality. It has devastated countless lives and destroyed families, churches, communities, and even nations.[5] 99

6. How can we support each other as a body of believers as we live into this holy calling?

[5] Barton, Bruce B., and Grant R. Osborne. *1 & 2 Thessalonians: Life Application Commentary.* Tyndale House Publishers, 1999. 57

> **"** Grace transforms our understanding of sexual ethics. It's not merely about following rules but about recognizing that sexual wholeness is part of a broader vision of human flourishing. It is living in a way that aligns with God's best for us, empowered by His grace.[6] **"**

7. God isn't calling us to live in this way out of fear but to provide a way for us to flourish. How can sexual wholeness allow for a flourishing life?

8. How is sexual wholeness connected to health within the body of Christ —the church?

[6] Bessey, Sarah. *Out of Sorts: Making Peace with an Evolving Faith*. Howard Books, 2015.

Reflection: We have so many ways to learn from each other—different life experiences, stages of life, mistakes, and successes. What have you learned from others about holy living? About wholeness and flourishing?

_____

_____

_____

_____

_____

_____

_____

9. How can our communal holy living be an example to those who don't yet know Christ?

10. In **verses 9-10**, Paul praised them for how they love one another and urged them to love even more. "There is always more to learn about love, always more depth to be plumbed, always more ways to show love. Paul wanted them to understand that love was not an end achieved once and for all but a continual process."[7] How can we continually grow in our love for one another?

[7] Barton, Bruce B., and Grant R. Osborne. _1 & 2 Thessalonians: Life Application Commentary._ Tyndale House Publishers, 1999. 61

11. Paul pointed out that their love was taught to them by God Himself. What have you learned about love from God?

Reflection: Pause and take some time to ask the Holy Spirit to teach you more about growing in love. Pay attention to the people who come to mind. Pay attention to areas of needed repentance or forgiveness. Pay attention to God's creativity as He continues to teach you and give you new abilities and ways of loving each other.

_____

_____

_____

_____

_____

_____

12. In **verses 11-12** Paul switched gears slightly. What did he instruct the believers to do and why?

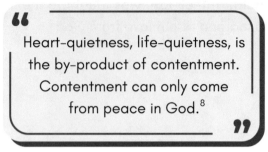

> **"** Heart-quietness, life-quietness, is the by-product of contentment. Contentment can only come from peace in God.[8] **"**

13. What does "living quietly" mean to you in your life?

14. How have you seen this kind of living, as believers at Salem Alliance, further our vision for Salem to be a city at peace with God?

15. How could living a quiet, holy life—out of reverence and worship—be intriguing to those who don't yet know Christ?

[8] Gupta, Nijay K. *1-2 Thessalonians: A New Covenant Commentary*. Cascade Books, 2016. 90

[9] "The redeemed, grace-rich people of God do not need to add extra noise to a noisy world. To live 'quietly' does not mean to sequester yourself, to step out of the world (see **1 Corinthians 5:9-10**). Rather, it is to respond to your God-given vocation and feel comfortable in your own skin and place in the world, such that your focus is not on being so loud about yourself that you get the right attention and boost your reputation up in the right ways in public." Gupta, Nijay K. *1-2 Thessalonians: A New Covenant Commentary*. Cascade Books, 2016. 90

16. In **1 Thessalonians 4:13-18**, Paul turned his attention to those who have lost someone to death. How would you describe Paul's encouragement to them?[10]

Reflection: Think of people in your life who are grieving the loss of a loved one. Take some time to pray for them. Take some time to grieve for them. If appropriate, write them a note of encouragement or reach out to them.

_____

_____

_____

_____

_____

_____

_____

_____

[10] "Paul wanted the Thessalonians to understand that death is not the end. When Christ returns, all believers—dead and alive—will be reunited, never to suffer or die again. Believers need not grieve as others do who have no hope. Paul recognized that the death of loved ones naturally results in grieving, but when Christians grieve for Christians who have died, there is a difference. Their grief is not hopeless." Barton, Bruce B., and Grant R. Osborne. *1 & 2 Thessalonians: Life Application Commentary.* Tyndale House Publishers, 1999. 63-64

17. How does the return of Christ[11] encourage you as you think about the future?[12]

[11]"Chapter four verse seventeen has been the subject of much attention because of two words: 'caught up' (*harpazo*) and 'meeting' (*apantesis*). As for the former, this is where we get the language and idea of 'the rapture' which has been popularized as an eschatological idea from the Left Behind books and movies. The word 'rapture' is taken from a Latin translation (*raptio*) of the word Paul uses here for 'caught up' (*harpazo*). The idea behind 'rapture' theology is that Jesus' return (the first of two future appearances) involves a secret snatching away of believers from earth. However, nothing in Paul's words here in **1 Thessalonians 4:17** leads us to believe that the appearance of Jesus is anything but public, visible, and loud." Gupta, Nijay K. *1-2 Thessalonians: A New Covenant Commentary*. Cascade Books, 2016. 96

[12]"Paul's point was not to give his readers a timeline or a literal description of how all the end-times events would fit together. Instead, he wanted to reassure the Thessalonians that their fellow believers who had died would not miss out on Christ's return and eternal kingdom." Barton, Bruce B., and Grant R. Osborne. *1 & 2 Thessalonians: Life Application Commentary*. Tyndale House Publishers, 1999. 68

Engage

As we go through these letters together, you will notice they are written to a community, not an individual. Paul was encouraging and instructing a group of people who were learning, growing, and enduring together.

As you read and study through 1-2 Thessalonians, think of ways to engage with your current community both through connection and encouragement. Each week, choose one thing from this list to practice as we continue to live out our future hope together.

- Write a note of gratitude or encouragement. Make plans to mail it or send it digitally.

- Ask God to put one person on your heart for prayer. Ask Him, what is on your heart for _____? Then notice any Scriptures, thoughts, or images that come to mind. You may want to share what you prayed and heard with them.

- Go to the Salem Alliance website and refresh your memory about the multiple ways we love and serve each other and our community. Choose a particular ministry to pray for. Consider writing an encouragement card to the point person or leader of that ministry. Pay attention to any ways God might be nudging you to engage with one of the ministries that you see. Use the QR Code below to access the website.

- Take a prayer walk. Ask God to put prayers of blessings on your heart as you walk through a particular neighborhood or area. Also pay attention to any ways that God might be nudging you to engage in acts of service in those areas.

Prayer

Spend time in prayer asking God to help you live a life of worship, to grow in love for others, and to hold fast to the hope of Jesus' return. You may consider using the prayer below as a guide:

Oh Lord, grant me a heart that overflows with love—a love that mirrors the boundless affection You have for all your creation.
Help me be a messenger of peace in every corner of my world; to show compassion, patience, and joy. In every encounter, may Your light shine through me, transforming shadows into warmth and understanding.
As I journey through the winding paths of time, anchor my soul in the hope of Your promised return. Let the anticipation of that holy reunion infuse my days with purpose, holy living, and unwavering faith.
Teach me to live with eyes turned toward the heavens, yet grounded in love for the earth and its weary travelers. Help us to grieve well with each other as we hope for heaven. Amen.

Sermon Notes

PRAYER REQUESTS

Faith, Hope, and Love
Lesson 5
1 Thessalonians 5

Before you begin, start by reading the fifth chapter of 1 Thessalonians.

In this, the last chapter of Paul's first letter to the Thessalonians, he wrapped up by reminding them that they must live in readiness—clothed in faith, hope, and love. He also offered practical advice on living peacefully, building each other up, and living holy lives as they waited for Christ. The first few verses of chapter five continue the conversation from chapter four about the Lord's return.

1. While Paul continued to emphasize that the day of the Lord's return will come unexpectedly (**5:2**), how did he encourage them? (**5:4-5**)

   How does this truth, which is also true about your identity, encourage you?

2. What challenges did Paul then give the Thessalonians? (**5:6-8**)

3. In his letter to the Ephesians, Paul extended a similar call:

Ephesians 6:11-13

11 Put on all of God's armor so that you will be able to stand firm against all strategies of the devil. 12 For we are not fighting against flesh-and-blood enemies, but against evil rulers and authorities of the unseen world, against mighty powers in this dark world, and against evil spirits in the heavenly places.
13 Therefore, put on every piece of God's armor so you will be able to resist the enemy in the time of evil. Then after the battle you will still be standing firm.

From **1 Thessalonians 5:6-8** and **Ephesians 6:11-13** above, what does it mean to be spiritually alert and on guard in your life?

> "Paul simply emphasizes that the key to vanquishing their fears lies in the power of these virtues [being spiritually alert and on guard] rather than any kind of preparation based on knowing dates and times.[1]"

4. How can being spiritually alert and on guard help to diminish your fears about the future?

[1] Gupta, Nijay K. *1-2 Thessalonians: A New Covenant Commentary.* Cascade Books, 2016. 90

5. While we reflect on what it means to be spiritually alert and on guard, we must remember that we can do so because of the power of the Holy Spirit within us. It is not in our own power that we stand strong, rather we stand strong because of our strong Protector. Read the following passages and underline what you notice about God.

Psalm 91:1-7

1 Those who live in the shelter of the Most High will find rest in the shadow of the Almighty.
2 This I declare about the LORD He alone is my refuge, my place of safety; he is my God, and I trust him.
3 For he will rescue you from every trap and protect you from deadly disease.
4 He will cover you with his feathers. He will shelter you with his wings. His faithful promises are your armor and protection.
5 Do not be afraid of the terrors of the night, nor the arrow that flies in the day.
6 Do not dread the disease that stalks in darkness, nor the disaster that strikes at midday.
7 Though a thousand fall at your side, though ten thousand are dying around you, these evils will not touch you.

Psalm 121

1 I look up to the mountains—does my help come from there?
2 My help comes from the LORD, who made heaven and earth!
3 He will not let you stumble; the one who watches over you will not slumber.
4 Indeed, he who watches over Israel never slumbers or sleeps.
5 The LORD himself watches over you! The LORD stands beside you as your protective shade.
6 The sun will not harm you by day, nor the moon at night.
7 The LORD keeps you from all harm and watches over your life.
8 The LORD keeps watch over you as you come and go, both now and forever.

See also: **Psalms 18, 23, 27, and 46**

Reflection: Meditate on what God is pointing out to you about His character as our protector. List the things that are grabbing your attention.

_____

_____

_____

_____

_____

_____

_____

As we return to **1 Thessalonians 5**, we note that in the last few verses of his encouragement Paul wrote:

"9 For God chose to save us through our Lord Jesus Christ, not to pour out his anger on us. 10 Christ died for us so that, whether we are dead or alive when he returns, we can live with him forever."

And then, Paul exhorts the Thessalonians to encourage one another with these same truths.

> **"** As you near the end of a long race, your legs ache, your throat burns, and your whole body cries out for you to stop. This is when friends and fans are most valuable. Their encouragement helps you push through the pain to the finish line.[2] **"**

6. How can you encourage someone else in faith, love, and hope this week?

Paul often concluded his letters with a series of final instructions, but we would be remiss if we either discredited them as obvious, or to the other extreme, made them a rigid rule book. "Most of the Gentile churches to which Paul ministered would have benefited from all kinds of general advice about holiness, purity, peace, and love."[3] As do we.

7. What guidance does Paul offer in **1 Thessalonians 5:12-13**?

Who is a spiritual leader you could encourage and pray for this week?

8. What are the next five pieces of advice from Paul? (**5:14-15**)

We can see from his advice that Paul was specific about understanding each person and the unique ways to interact with them (warn the lazy, take tender care of the weak, etc.).
One theologian summarizes Paul's advice in this way: "The key to [living this way] is sensitivity: sensing the condition of each person and offering the appropriate remedy for each situation. You can't effectively help until you know the problem. You can't apply the medicine until you know where the wound is."[4]

[3] Gupta, Nijay K. *1-2 Thessalonians: A New Covenant Commentary.* Cascade Books, 2016. 111
[4] *Life Application Study Bible: NLT.* Zondervan; Tyndale House Publishers, Inc, 2019. 2046

9. In what ways do you find the summary on the previous page to be true? Can you think of some examples to share?

10. How can you cultivate peace and patience in your relationships?

11. "The next three verses [**1 Thessalonians 5:16-18**] give three simple ingredients that believers ought to daily mix into their lives: joy, prayer, and thanks. When these three qualities are present, believers will be vibrant witnesses to a needy world."[5] How have you seen this to be true in your life? In our community?

> ❝ For three things I thank God every day of my life: thanks that he has [graciously granted] me knowledge of his works; deep thanks that he has set in my darkness the lamp of faith; deep deepest thanks that I have another life to look forward to—a life joyous with light and flowers and heavenly song.
> Helen Keller ❞

[5] Bruce B., and Grant R. Osborne. *1 & 2 Thessalonians: Life Application Commentary*. Tyndale House Publishers, 1999. 82

Reflection: Take some time for simple gratitude. List some of the things you are most grateful for these days.

_____

_____

_____

_____

_____

_____

_____

_____

12. What is the difference between thanking God <u>for</u> everything and thanking God <u>in</u> everything? (**5:18**)

Do you think this distinction is important? Why or why not?

13. What are Paul's final words of advice? (**5:19-22**)

14. Which of these final words stand out to you as an area where God might be challenging you to grow?

> **"** The conduct Paul has been prescribing [throughout his letter to the Thessalonians] is impossible from a human standpoint. People will not naturally rejoice always, pray continually, and give thanks in every situation (**5:16-18**), nor can they keep away from all evil (**5:22**). But Paul did not expect the Thessalonian believers to do this in their own strength.[6] **"**

1 Thessalonians 5:23-24

23 Now may the God of peace make you holy in every way, and may your whole spirit and soul and body be kept blameless until our Lord Jesus Christ comes again. 24 God will make this happen, for he who calls you is faithful.

15. In what ways does this quote and Paul's prayer encourage you as you live a life of faith, hope, and love?

How can living a holy life of faith, hope, and love—especially in community with one another—bear witness to those who don't yet know Christ?

[6] Bruce B., and Grant R. Osborne. *1 & 2 Thessalonians: Life Application Commentary.* Tyndale House Publishers, 1999. 89

Engage

As we go through these letters together, you will notice they are written to a community, not an individual. Paul was encouraging and instructing a group of people who were learning, growing, and enduring together.

As you read and study through 1-2 Thessalonians, think of ways to engage with your current community both through connection and encouragement. Each week, choose one thing from this list to practice as we continue to live out our future hope together.

- Write a note of gratitude or encouragement. Make plans to mail it or send it digitally.

- Ask God to put one person on your heart for prayer. Ask Him, what is on your heart for _____? Then notice any Scriptures, thoughts, or images that come to mind. You may want to share what you prayed and heard with them.

- Go to the Salem Alliance website and refresh your memory about the multiple ways we love and serve each other and our community. Choose a particular ministry to pray for. Consider writing an encouragement card to the point person or leader of that ministry. Pay attention to any ways God might be nudging you to engage with one of the ministries that you see. Use the QR Code below to access the website.

- Take a prayer walk. Ask God to put prayers of blessings on your heart as you walk through a particular neighborhood or area. Also pay attention to any ways that God might be nudging you to engage in acts of service in those areas.

Prayer

End your time by praying together, asking God to help you be spiritually alert, to clothe you in faith, hope, and love, and to give you the grace to live in peace and holiness as you wait for Christ's return.

Together, pray through each of these three words, slowly, leaving room for God to respond.

Lord, we ask You to clothe us with faith.

Together, pause for silence in order to notice how God responds. Pay attention to any Scriptures, situations, images, songs, etc. that come to mind. Allow God to prompt your thoughts.

Lord, we ask You to clothe us with hope.

Pause to notice how God responds.

Lord, we ask You to clothe us with love.

Pause to notice how God responds.

Sermon Notes

PRAYER REQUESTS

Justice Is Coming
Lesson 6
2 Thessalonians 1

Before you begin, start by reading the first chapter of 2 Thessalonians.

"Paul wrote this letter from Corinth less than a year after he wrote 1 Thessalonians. ... While the purpose of Paul's first letter was to comfort the Thessalonians with the assurance of Christ's second coming, the purpose of this second letter was to correct false teaching about the second coming." [1]

"In many ways, 2 Thessalonians is a re-expression of 1 Thessalonians, repeating many of the earlier text's themes, arguments, and sometimes even its wording. In fact the opening greeting of 2 Thessalonians is almost identical to **1 Thessalonians 1:1-2**." [2]

1. The church at Thessalonica was still experiencing great suffering and persecution.[3] What do you learn about their experience from **1:3-4**?[4]

2. How have you seen God grow your faith and love during difficult times?

[1] Bruce B., and Grant R. Osborne. *1 & 2 Thessalonians: Life Application Commentary.* Tyndale House Publishers, 1999. 103

[2] Gupta, Nijay K. *1-2 Thessalonians: A New Covenant Commentary.* Cascade Books, 2016. 119

[3] "The word *diogmois*, 'persecutions,' refers to assaults made on the believers because of their faith in Christ; *thlipsesin*, 'hardships,' is a more general word for difficulties in life (pressures or burdens). Bruce B., and Grant R. Osborne. *1 & 2 Thessalonians: Life Application Commentary.* Tyndale House Publishers, 1999. 109

[4] "The word translated 'flourishing' (*hyperauxenei*) is used only here in the New Testament and speaks of the type of growth a healthy plant makes. The picture is of internal growth, like that of an oak tree. The word translated 'growing' (*pleonazei*) is also a strong verb picturing something that spreads out or disperses widely —like floodwaters." Bruce B., and Grant R. Osborne. *1 & 2 Thessalonians: Life Application Commentary.* Tyndale House Publishers, 1999. 107

3. "In **2 Thessalonians 1:3-5**, Paul seems to link suffering with being worthy of the kingdom of God. At the very least, Paul appears to be reflecting on a positive feature of persecution from the world in the life of believers. For many Christians, back then but also today, this can be counter-intuitive. Isn't Jesus supposed to make my life better and easier?"[5]   [6]

   Where have you seen this type of thinking in your own life?

4. **Verse 5** can cause some interpretive challenges. One scholar interprets it this way: "Here is how I understand what Paul is saying in **1:5**: You Thessalonians are suffering and you wonder, 'who is pulling the strings up there in heaven? Is God in control? Is he punishing us? Is he trustworthy?' I say to you, God is in control and he is acting according to his good pleasure and looking after you at the same time. The afflictions you are suffering are not a negative reflection of your worth and value to God..."

   The scholar goes on to ask, what if you considered suffering as a privilege? What if you lived into suffering with the idea that God would let you represent His kingdom and that, with His help and the Holy Spirit, He trusts you to rise above the persecution in faithfulness and hope.

   How could this scholar's interpretation help us understand that suffering is not a sign of God's displeasure?

[5] Gupta, Nijay K. *1-2 Thessalonians: A New Covenant Commentary.* Cascade Books, 2016. 128

[6] "The idea is neither that sufferings earn salvation, nor that God desires to see his people suffer. Rather, we often misunderstand what it means to be a Christian if we think accepting Jesus gets us 'off the hook' of any suffering or pain." Gupta, Nijay K. *1-2 Thessalonians: A New Covenant Commentary.* Cascade Books, 2016. 128

[7] Gupta, Nijay K. *1-2 Thessalonians: A New Covenant Commentary.* Cascade Books, 2016. 124-125

5. How do you typically respond to suffering?

How could you continue to grow in the knowledge that the way we endure suffering could be a way to represent God's Kingdom to those around us?

6. Take some time to notice what the following verses teach us about suffering:

Luke 6:22-23

22 What blessings await you when people hate you and exclude you and mock you and curse you as evil because you follow the Son of Man. 23 When that happens, be happy! Yes, leap for joy! For a great reward awaits you in heaven. And remember, their ancestors treated the ancient prophets that same way.

Romans 8:17

And since we are his children, we are his heirs. In fact, together with Christ we are heirs of God's glory. But if we are to share his glory, we must also share his suffering.

Acts 5:41

The apostles left the high council rejoicing that God had counted them worthy to suffer disgrace for the name of Jesus.

Acts 14:22

They encouraged them to continue in the faith, reminding them that we must suffer many hardships to enter the Kingdom of God.

How do these passages help us understand suffering from a Christian perspective?

7. What do you notice about God's justice from **2 Thessalonians 1:7-10**, both for those who are righteous and those who are not?

8. In these verses (**7-9**), Paul mentioned those who will be separated from God's presence. How does this passage stir your heart for those who don't yet know Christ?

9. How can you be more intentional about sharing the Gospel with others, knowing what's at stake?

> " God is just—his very nature is justice (see **Deuteronomy 32:4; 2 Chronicles 19:7**). God will act with complete justice when he punishes sinners, but only after providing a way for people not to be punished. [8] "

10. How does knowing that God's justice will prevail give you hope? (See **2 Peter 3:9** as you answer.)

11. "God's relief doesn't always come the moment we want it, but God knows the best time to act. When you feel as though God has forgotten you in your troubles, remember that he has set a day for restoring justice."[9] How do you handle waiting and trusting in God's timing? How has this understanding helped you through past struggles?

[8] Bruce B., and Grant R. Osborne. *1 & 2 Thessalonians: Life Application Commentary.* Tyndale House Publishers, 1999. 110

[9] Bruce B., and Grant R. Osborne. *1 & 2 Thessalonians: Life Application Commentary.* Tyndale House Publishers, 1999. 112

Paul ends this part of his letter with another prayer in **2 Thessalonians 1:11-12**:

11 So we keep on praying for you, asking our God to enable you to live a life worthy of his call. May he give you the power to accomplish all the good things your faith prompts you to do. 12 Then the name of our Lord Jesus will be honored because of the way you live, and you will be honored along with him. This is all made possible because of the grace of our God and Lord, Jesus Christ.

Reflection: Personalize Paul's prayer. First, pray it for someone you know. Pray slowly enough that the Holy Spirit can prompt you with some specifics for that person. Then pray for yourself in the same way.

_____

_____

_____

_____

_____

_____

_____

Engage

As we go through these letters together, you will notice they are written to a community, not an individual. Paul was encouraging and instructing a group of people who were learning, growing, and enduring together.

As you read and study through 1-2 Thessalonians, think of ways to engage with your current community both through connection and encouragement. Each week, choose one thing from this list to practice as we continue to live out our future hope together.

- Write a note of gratitude or encouragement. Make plans to mail it or send it digitally.

- Ask God to put one person on your heart for prayer. Ask Him, what is on your heart for _____? Then notice any Scriptures, thoughts, or images that come to mind. You may want to share what you prayed and heard with them.

- Go to the Salem Alliance website and refresh your memory about the multiple ways we love and serve each other and our community. Choose a particular ministry to pray for. Consider writing an encouragement card to the point person or leader of that ministry. Pay attention to any ways God might be nudging you to engage with one of the ministries that you see. Use the QR Code below to access the website.

- Take a prayer walk. Ask God to put prayers of blessings on your heart as you walk through a particular neighborhood or area. Also pay attention to any ways that God might be nudging you to engage in acts of service in those areas.

Prayer

Spend time in prayer, thanking God for His justice, asking Him to help you live a life worthy of His call, and praying for those who don't yet know Him.

Heavenly Father, we thank You for Your promises of justice and for the assurance that our suffering is not in vain. Help us to grow in faith and love, to endure with perseverance, and to live lives worthy of Your calling. May Your justice be a source of hope and comfort, and may we be diligent in prayer, seeking Your guidance and strength. In Jesus' name, Amen.

Sermon Notes

PRAYER REQUESTS

Don't Be Fooled
Lesson 7
2 Thessalonians 2

Before you begin, start by reading the second chapter of 2 Thessalonians.

In this chapter, Paul addressed the Thessalonians' concerns about the Day of the Lord, urging them not to be fooled by false teachings. He reminded them that a great rebellion will precede Christ's return, but God will ultimately be victorious. Paul encouraged them to stand firm in the truth and to be comforted by the eternal hope they have in Christ.

1. Paul continued his second letter by bringing clarity to his teachings from his first letter, how would you describe what he was clarifying? (**2:1-12**)

   What questions rise up in you as you read **2 Thessalonians 2:1-12**?

2. Paul warned the Thessalonians not to be easily shaken or fooled by false teachings about Christ's return.[1] How can you guard against being misled or fooled by false doctrines?

[1] "... Troublemakers in Thessalonica had sowed the seed of fear that this Thessalonian church was facing judgment associated with the Day of the Lord, and it did not take much to whip them into a frenzy." Gupta, Nijay K. *1-2 Thessalonians: A New Covenant Commentary*. Cascade Books, 2016. 132

3. Are there particular sources of media or information that may be stirring you up in ways that are contrary to the peace that comes from the Holy Spirit? What are some ways you could realign your focus to better experience the Holy Spirit's peace?

> **"** In the midst of a culture saturated with false teachings, the call to discernment is not just about avoiding error but about deeply understanding and embodying the truth of God's Word.[2] **"**

4. What practices help you stay rooted in the truth of God's Word? Share and discuss these with your group. How will you implement them in the coming week?

[2] Leach, Tara Beth. *Emboldened: A Vision for Empowering Women in the Church.* Zondervan, 2019.

5. The Thessalonian church was concerned that they had somehow missed the coming of the Day of the Lord—Christ's return. Paul was using this letter to clarify that the day had not yet come and that there would be obvious signs. One of the main signs would be a man of lawlessness. How is the man of lawlessness described? (**2:3-4**; **9-12**)

> ❝ Paul does not specifically identify the Lawless One, but the language he uses for him is reminiscent of notorious enemies in Israel's past. ... But for Paul the Lawless One is a person yet to come in the future. Christians have speculated (sometimes wildly) regarding the identity of this person. All we can gather from Paul's brief remarks is that he will be a grandiose rebel in league with Satan (**2 Thessalonians 2:9**). Whether he is superhuman or mortal is unclear from the little Paul writes, but it could be that even Paul did not know the answer to this. ... Given the metaphor-laden nature of this entire section (**2:3-12**), we should be wary of pressing for too many details. Paul is not trying to work out the specifics for the Thessalonians, but to inform them of a great dividing line between the wicked and the righteous, and that there will be a great rebellion where the Lawless One will try to dethrone God himself.❞

6. What will God's response to the man of lawlessness be? (**2:8**)

[3]Gupta, Nijay K. *1-2 Thessalonians: A New Covenant Commentary*. Cascade Books, 2016. 134-135

7. "When it comes to **2 Thessalonians 2:8**, the important thing to note here is that ... there is no battle. There is no moment when it looks like Jesus might lose. He appears in glory and power and vanquishes the Lawless One effortlessly."[4] How does this passage bring you comfort, knowing that God is in control and that evil will not have the final say?

8. Jump down to **verse 15**. Paul said, *"with all these things in mind..."* referring to **2:13-14**. What things are they to keep in mind?

9. What did Paul believe that keeping those things in mind would help them do? (**2:15**)

10. Why is standing firm and keeping a strong grip on truthful teaching (not being fooled) so important—both then and now?

[4]Gupta, Nijay K. *1-2 Thessalonians: A New Covenant Commentary.* Cascade Books, 2016. 138

Reflection: One way to test whether something is from God is to meditate on the fruit of the Spirit. Teachings and beliefs from the Spirit will reflect and result in these fruits. Ask yourself: does holding onto this teaching produce love, joy, peace, patience, kindness, goodness, faithfulness, gentleness, and self-control? As you reflect, make note of what God is bringing to mind.

_____

_____

_____

_____

_____

_____

11. "The central problem amongst the Thessalonians was that they were paralyzed with fear about what is yet to come. The specifics change in every generation, but many Christians today are also worried about the future. Paul does not preach the hope of an easy future—in some ways things will get worse before they get better; but he still encourages believers to put their hope in God and trust that God will lead his people towards a good end."[4] As N.T. Wright suggests, "The hope of the future is grounded in the faithfulness of God, not in our ability to predict or control."

How can we continue to hold on to hope in the face of an unknown future?

[4]Gupta, Nijay K. 1-2 Thessalonians: A New Covenant Commentary. Cascade Books, 2016. 143

12. What are practical ways to share the hope of God's ultimate victory with those who are anxious or fearful about the future—both with people who know Christ and those who don't yet know Him?

13. While Paul shared about hope for the future, he also reminded the Thessalonians about the promises they had for their current day. We are not called to just focus on the future, but also on the reality that the Holy Spirit lives with us now. How does hope for the future influence the reality you live in today?

14. Paul closed this chapter with a prayer and blessing. Read **2 Thessalonians 2:16-17**. What does it look like in your life for God to comfort and strengthen you?

How does this prayer resonate with you in your current circumstances?

15. Who in your life could use encouragement to stand firm in their faith? How could you encourage them this week?

Pause and ask God for His comfort and strength—in every good thing you do and say.

Engage

As we go through these letters together, you will notice they are written to a community, not an individual. Paul was encouraging and instructing a group of people who were learning, growing, and enduring together.

As you read and study through 1-2 Thessalonians, think of ways to engage with your current community both through connection and encouragement. Each week, choose one thing from this list to practice as we continue to live out our future hope together.

- Write a note of gratitude or encouragement. Make plans to mail it or send it digitally.

- Ask God to put one person on your heart for prayer. Ask Him, what is on your heart for _____? Then notice any Scriptures, thoughts, or images that come to mind. You may want to share what you prayed and heard with them.

- Go to the Salem Alliance website and refresh your memory about the multiple ways we love and serve each other and our community. Choose a particular ministry to pray for. Consider writing an encouragement card to the point person or leader of that ministry. Pay attention to any ways God might be nudging you to engage with one of the ministries that you see. Use the QR Code below to access the website.

- Take a prayer walk. Ask God to put prayers of blessings on your heart as you walk through a particular neighborhood or area. Also pay attention to any ways that God might be nudging you to engage in acts of service in those areas.

Prayer

End your time in prayer, asking God to help you stand firm in the truth, to give you hope in the face of uncertainty, and to comfort those who need encouragement.

Gracious God, grant us the courage to stand firm in our faith, unwavering in the face of uncertainty and the allure of deception. May Your truth be our anchor and guide as we navigate the complexities and difficulties of life. Teach and empower us to encourage and support one another, helping each other remain steadfast in the knowledge of your eternal comfort and hope. Amen.

Sermon Notes

PRAYER REQUESTS

Active Waiting

Lesson 8

2 Thessalonians 3

Before you begin, start by reading the third chapter of 2 Thessalonians.

Paul concluded this letter by encouraging the Thessalonians to be active in their waiting for Christ's return. He prayed for the spread of the Gospel and for protection from evil. He also urged them not to be idle, but to work hard and live lives that benefit others.

1. In **2 Thessalonians 3:1-2**, Paul asked for prayer that the message of the Lord would spread rapidly and be honored. "Paul's request for prayer reflects the interconnectedness of mission and the power of intercessory prayer. The advance of the gospel is not merely a matter of human effort but requires divine intervention and support through prayer."[1]

   How can you pray for missionaries, local church outreach efforts, or personal relationships where the Gospel can be shared?

2. In what ways do you, or could you, participate in helping the Gospel reach others?

[1] Adeney, Miriam. *Kingdom Without Borders: The Untold Story of Global Christianity*. IVP Books, 2009.

3. Spend some time in prayer, together with your group, for the spread of the Gospel.

   Discuss some specific strategies for integrating Gospel-focused prayer into your ongoing daily routine.

4. Paul also prayed for protection from evil and for the Thessalonians to have a full understanding of God's love and endurance (**2 Thessalonians 3:3-5**). How do you see God guarding you from evil in your life?

5. In **2 Thessalonians 3:6-13** Paul warned against idleness and meddling in other people's lives. He encouraged the Thessalonians to work hard and live lives that benefited others. How can you actively wait for Christ's return by serving others and working hard in your daily life?

6. "Paul clarifies here that the issue is not capability to work but desire to do one's part. Paul does not mean that the community should not care for those who are not able to provide for themselves physically. Rather, he is warning against the rebellious attitude that holds oneself higher than those around one. The significance of the individual's actions and choices on the community is coming into view."[2]

In what ways can we guard against a rebellious attitude and ensure that our actions contribute positively to the well-being of our community?

7. "Paul's teachings on work and discipline reveal a vision for Christian life that is actively engaged with the world. This call to a disciplined life is not merely about personal piety but about shaping a community that reflects God's justice and love."[3] It's obvious that Paul is saying we aren't alone in this journey.

Where in your life are you walking with a community of people in this way?

How can living this way point people to Christ?

[2] Skeen, Jude as quoted in Gupta, Nijay K. *1-2 Thessalonians: A New Covenant Commentary*. Cascade Books, 2016. 150

[3] Rossing, Barbara R. *The Rapture Exposed: The Message of Hope in the Book of Revelation*. Basic Books, 2004.

8. How do Paul's instructions in **2 Thessalonians 3:14-15** balance the need for maintaining church discipline with the call to treat those who are in error with grace and compassion?

9. Paul ended his letter with a prayer. The title he used for God in his prayer was "Lord of Peace." What does it mean to you for God to be described as the "Lord of Peace"?

How does this title influence your understanding of God's character and His involvement in your life?

10. Paul prays for peace "at all times and in every way." How does this prayer encourage you to view peace in relation to both everyday challenges and significant trials?

11. How can you be a conduit of God's peace to others in your community?

12. How can peace be part of our active waiting?

Reflection: God has given Salem Alliance a vision of peace for our city. Take some time to ask God about this. Invite Him to bring peace to your life and home. Invite Him to bring peace to your neighborhood. Invite Him to bring peace to our city. As you do, pay attention to what God prompts in you. Make note of it here.

_____

_____

_____

_____

_____

_____

Engage

As we have gone through each chapter of these two letters, we have engaged with the practice of interacting in our current communities both through connection and encouragement. Each week, you chose one way to live it out. How was this process for you? Take some time to reflect on the questions below.

- Where did I feel delight as I engaged in these practices?

- Where did I notice resistance?

- How would I describe the connection and communion with God and others I experienced through these practices?

- Where do I see evidence of myself becoming a person of Christ-like love through these practices?

- Share your experience with your group.

Prayer

End your time in prayer together. Use the words of St. Francis as we invite God to bring peace to our community and our world.

Lord, make me an instrument of your peace.
Where there is hatred, let me sow love;
where there is injury, pardon;
where there is doubt, faith;
where there is despair, hope;
where there is darkness, light;
and where there is sadness, joy.
O Divine Master, grant that I may not so much seek
to be consoled as to console;
to be understood as to understand;
to be loved as to love.
For it is in giving that we receive;
it is in pardoning that we are pardoned;
and it is in dying that we are born to eternal life.
Amen.

Sermon Notes

PRAYER REQUESTS

Made in United States
Troutdale, OR
10/08/2024

23575485R00051